How To Use This Study Guide

This five-lesson study guide corresponds to *"How To Have a Happy Marriage" With Rick Renner* (Renner TV). Each lesson in this study guide covers a topic that is addressed during the program series, with questions and references supplied to draw you deeper into your own private study of the Scriptures on this subject.

To derive the most benefit from this study guide, consider the following:

First, watch or listen to the program prior to working through the corresponding lesson in this guide. (Programs can also be viewed at **renner.org** by clicking on the Media/Archives links or on our Renner Ministries YouTube channel.)

Second, take the time to look up the scriptures included in each lesson. Prayerfully consider their application to your own life.

Third, use a journal or notebook to make note of your answers to each lesson's Study Questions and Practical Application challenges.

Fourth, invest specific time in prayer and in the Word of God to consult with the Holy Spirit. Write down the scriptures or insights He reveals to you.

Finally, take action! Whatever the Lord tells you to do according to His Word, do it.

For added insights on this subject, it is recommended that you obtain Rick Renner's *Renner Interpretive Version (RIV) of First and Second Peter* and Denise Renner's *Who Stole Cinderella? — The Art of 'Happily Ever After'*. You may also select from Rick's other available resources by placing your order at **renner.org** or by calling 1-800-742-5593.

TOPIC

Is Christ in Your Marriage?

SCRIPTURES

1. **Ecclesiastes 4:9** — Two are better than one; because they have a good reward for their labour.

2. **Ecclesiastes 4:10** — For if they fall, the one will lift up his fellow: but woe to him that is alone when he falleth; for he hath not another to help him up.

3. **Ecclesiastes 4:11-12** — Again, if two lie together, then they have heat: but how can one be warm alone? And if one prevail against him, two shall withstand him; and a threefold cord is not quickly broken.

GREEK WORDS

No Greek words were shown on the TV program.

SYNOPSIS

The five lessons in this study on *How To Have a Happy Marriage* will focus on the following topics:

- Is Christ in Your Marriage?
- Does Your Marriage Have Purpose?
- Can You Shut the Door to Strife?
- How Important Is Grace to Marriage?
- Should You Control Your Mouth?

The emphasis of this lesson:

Rick and Denise are celebrating 44 years of marriage in 2025, and in this lesson, they share how their happy marriage began. Before they met, each of them had dreams they were passionately pursuing. When God revealed His will for them to become a married couple and serve Him together for the rest of their lives, they each had a decision to

A Note From Rick Renner

I am on a personal quest to see a "revival of the Bible" so people can establish their lives on a firm foundation that will stand strong and endure the test as end-time storm winds begin to intensify.

In order to experience a revival of the Bible in your personal life, it is important to take time each day to read, receive, and apply its truths to your life. James tells us that if we will continue in the perfect law of liberty — refusing to be forgetful hearers, but determined to be doers — we will be blessed in our ways. As you watch or listen to the programs in this series and work through this corresponding study guide, I trust you will search the Scriptures and allow the Holy Spirit to help you hear something new from God's Word that applies specifically to your life. I encourage you to be a doer of the Word He reveals to you. Whatever the cost, I assure you — it will be worth it.

> Thy words were found, and I did eat them;
> and thy word was unto me the joy and rejoicing of mine heart:
> for I am called by thy name, O Lord God of hosts.
> — Jeremiah 15:16

Your brother and friend in Jesus Christ,

Rick Renner

Unless otherwise indicated, all scripture quotations are taken from the *King James Version* of the Bible.

Scripture quotations marked (*AMPC*) are taken from the *Amplified® Bible, Classic Edition*. Copyright © 1954, 1958, 1962, 1964, 1965, 1987 by The Lockman Foundation. Used by permission. **www.Lockman.org**.

Scripture quotations taken from the New American Standard Bible® (*NASB*) Copyright © 1960, 1962, 1963, 1968, 1971, 1972, 1973, 1975, 1977, 1995 by The Lockman Foundation. Used by permission. **www.Lockman.org**.

Scripture quotations marked (*NKJV*) are taken from the *New King James Version®*. Copyright © 1982 by Thomas Nelson. Used by permission. All rights reserved.

Scripture quotations marked (*RIV*) are taken from *Renner Interpretive Version*. Copyright © 2021 by Rick Renner.

How To Have a Happy Marriage

Copyright © 2025 by Rick Renner
1814 W. Tacoma St.
Broken Arrow, OK 74012-1406

Published by Rick Renner Ministries
www.renner.org

ISBN 13: 978-1-6675-1347-8

eBook ISBN 13: 978-1-6675-1348-5

All rights reserved. No portion of this book may be reproduced or transmitted in any form or by any means — electronic, mechanical, photocopy, recording, scanning, or other — except for brief quotations in critical reviews or articles, without the prior written permission of the Publisher.

make. By yielding to His plan for their lives, united together, they started bringing forth eternal fruit from the very beginning. Christ was at the center of their marriage from day one, and He can be at the center of *yours* too!

A Relationship Born While Reaching People

When Rick was a young man, he decided he would never get married. He wanted to be single like the apostle Paul. He shared, "I just wanted to be committed and undistracted so I could serve the Lord freely. And I literally had no interest in girls or in the subject of marriage." As a young man, he found himself attending a little college church that he loved, because the people who attended were filled with the Spirit and dedicated to evangelism.

One day, Rick was sitting in church during a worship service when somebody in the back of the room began to sing a prophetic song. He wondered who it was and turned to see the source of the beautiful voice behind him. That was the first time Rick laid eyes on Denise Roberson. At the time, Denise was a student at the university, training to be a professional opera singer. But on that day, she began to sing prophetically and spontaneously by the Spirit, and her voice gripped him. Rick recalled:

> The first time I ever saw Denise, she was *obeying the Lord* and singing a prophetic song. After the service, I went back to meet her because I was so impressed with her voice. I'm *still* impressed with her voice! But from time to time, she would sing a prophetic song in that church.
>
> Denise and I were both committed to evangelism. One Saturday, we showed up at the church, and all of the teams were being dispatched to do evangelism. Denise and I ended up on the same team, and we went to a local nursing home. We went from room to room, until finally, at the end of one corridor, there was a man who was dealing with brain cancer. His name was Frank and we led him to the Lord. That was the first spiritual fruit of our relationship. *Our marriage, our relationship, was born while reaching people, born while preaching the Gospel and furthering God's Kingdom.*

From Friendship in the Lord to a Proposal

During this time, Denise was passionately pursuing a career in the opera. She later auditioned at the Metropolitan Opera in New York City and had a spectacular career in front of her. Then she and Rick got married. But before all that happened, Rick began to teach in the church in their little university town, and his gift began to be developed. He shared more of their testimony:

> I ended up attending a wedding, and Denise was there. It was during the summer break, and I had gone back to Tulsa to work during that time. I was just being friendly with Denise — I had no interest in her. I was just being polite, and I said to her that she looked very pretty. Then I said, 'You ought to come to Tulsa sometime and see me.'
>
> I did not mean a word of it. If I knew she was going to take me up on it, I would never have offered it. Like I said, I was just being polite. So I was in Tulsa for the summer, and the phone rang. It was Denise. She said, 'I'm going to come to Tulsa because you invited me.' When I hung the phone up, I thought, *What am I going to do with this girl for three days?*
>
> The next thing I knew, I was parked at the turnpike exit waiting for somebody to drop her off. I picked her up and I thought again, *What am I going to do with this girl for three days?* And in those three days, we drove around a lot. We went to church to hear Corrie Ten Boom speak. We sang a lot of hymns together because we didn't know each other, but we knew a lot of hymns. So we would drive, and we would sing. Then we would talk. She would talk about her future, and I would talk about my dreams.
>
> I found myself saying — still to this day, I can't believe that I said this — but we were having ice cream and I found myself saying, 'Denise, if I asked you to be my wife, would you marry me?' She said, 'If God called me to be your wife, then, of course.' At that time, Denise was looking for a husband. Her dream was to marry a preacher, not to be an opera singer. She felt a call to the ministry, and here was a young preacher right in front of her.

Wrestling With God's Will

Rick went on to share more about his and Denise's testimony:

> It looked like the two of us were being put together, but I didn't have a desire to be married. I had no interest in marriage at all. In fact, when that question came out of my mouth, I wished I could grab those words and take them back because before I knew it, I had proposed. I wasn't even twenty years old, and Denise was a little bit older than me. I thought, *What in the world have I done?*

> When the weekend was over, I took Denise back to the turnpike area. Somebody picked her up, and she went back to the university. For the summer, I continued working at my job. Denise later said that as she got out of the car that day, she heard wedding bells, and at that moment, she knew I was to be her husband.

> That summer, I wrote Denise a lot of letters, and the Lord began speaking to me prophetically about her. I still have all those early documents where the Lord spoke to me. But I could not deal with the issue of marriage because I was not interested in marriage. I was the man who was going to be undistracted, uncommitted to marriage, just committed solely to the Lord like the apostle Paul.

> At the end of the summer when I went back to the university, I blew the whole thing off as if it never happened. I ignored Denise. In fact, I actually said, 'Denise, can we please forget that I proposed? Can we erase that and move on?' I wanted things to be as if we never had that conversation.

> Denise thought I was a jerk. And actually what I did was what a jerk would do, but I was afraid. And I was young. Praise God that we didn't get married at that moment because I was not ready for that. Denise wasn't either. Several years went by, and I knew that I was in disobedience about marrying Denise. And during the time that I was in disobedience, Denise went to New York to continue in her pursuit of a career in the opera.

Denise Receives Her Call From the Lord

Denise shared her experiences from the time that she was waiting for God to bring her marriage partner to her. She said:

> I went to New York, and my teacher was amazing. He was a true opera singer. He sang in places in Europe, and he believed in me and believed in my voice. He took me to the Metropolitan Opera and the New York City Opera to audition. At the Metropolitan, I sang, and they said I was impressive, tall, and had major talent. They told me to come back in one year and sing for James Levine, who was the director of the Metropolitan Opera. At the New York City Opera, I auditioned for Beverly Sills.

> I was in the process of learning all the arias for a particular opera for my audition — *Macbeth* by Guiseppi Verdi. I was working so hard on those arias because they are difficult. It's a very difficult role to sing. I went to our little church for a service and as I was sitting there, the Holy Spirit said to me, 'I didn't call you to aspire to the Metropolitan Opera, but that the praises of God would come out of you, over this pipe, and give glory and honor to Me.'

> At that moment, I received my call from the Lord, so I changed my whole summer plan. I had a fully paid scholarship to an opera camp in Europe that summer, but I told my teacher I was not going. My teacher was not happy about this, and I told Rick about it. Rick was so sweet because he respected my talent and he said, 'Denise, I can't take your voice from the world.' But he didn't have to because the Lord called me to sing His praises. So I told that to Rick, and we began to pursue our relationship further.

A Wholehearted Commitment to Each Other and to the Lord

Rick continued to share the story from his perspective and explained how he finally became committed to pursuing the spouse God had called him to marry:

> Our relationship was confusing because it was on again, off again, on again, off again. But I proposed one more time, and I said, 'Denise, I'm so sorry that I was erratic the first time.' Denise cried

and cried. We were having breakfast together, and I said, 'Denise, I know that God has called you to be my wife. Would you please marry me? I want to love you as Christ loves the Church.' Then I left that breakfast and didn't call her again for a year. I got terrified again. The idea of getting married scared the wits out of me.

Finally I ended up in the hospital — very, very sick. I said to the Lord, 'What opened the door for this sickness?' And the Lord said, 'Your disobedience.' I said, 'What disobedience?' He said, 'I told you to marry Denise Roberson.' The Lord continued, 'I didn't give you the sickness, but you've opened the door to the devil because you are not in My will. And when you're not in My will, you experience bad things. You're sick because you're not doing what I told you to do, and you've opened a door for this sickness to attack you.'

Right then from my hospital bed, I picked up the phone and called Denise. In fact, I called her just at the right time because she was in a very vulnerable moment with another situation, and we just connected. Finally, the day came when we walked the aisle. Denise was so beautiful that day, and she found me very handsome. She sang to me, and I washed her feet. I got on my knees with a bucket of water, and I committed to the Lord, to Denise, and to the Body of Christ that I would serve her for the rest of our lives. And that began our marriage together.

A Purpose-Filled Life Is Important

Ecclesiastes 4:9 declares, "Two are better than one; because they have a good reward for their labour." As a young man *before* he got married, Rick didn't believe that. He thought he was sufficient by himself. But God told him that Denise was to be his wife. And the truth is that "two are better than one; because they have a good reward for their labour."

One reason marriages flounder is that two people just marry each other, and that's all there is — just the daily routine of life, but with another person present. Eventually, that's not enough and people become disappointed. They begin to feel frustrated, and they wonder, *Isn't there more to marriage than this?* Marriage needs to have a purpose. In fact, everything needs to have a purpose. Again, this verse says, "Two are better than one; because they have a good reward for their labour." When Rick and Denise look at their marriage, they can declare, "Look what the Lord has done through our labor together. It is amazing."

Ecclesiastes 4:10 then goes on to say, "For if they fall, the one will lift up his fellow: but woe to him that is alone when he falleth; for he hath not another to help him up." For 44 years, Rick and Denise have been helping each other while living out their purpose. No matter what they face, they are committed to helping one another succeed.

'A Threefold Cord Is Not Quickly Broken'

The marriage relationship is powerful! Ecclesiastes 4:11 and 12 admonish, "Again, if two lie together, then they have heat: but how can one be warm alone? And if one prevail against him, two shall withstand him…." When you are united with another person in marriage, you have spiritual power to stand against the enemy *together*.

The final part of verse 12 is foundational to marriage: "…And a threefold cord is not quickly broken." It's not just two people in marriage — it's three. A *threefold* cord is not quickly broken. From the very beginning of their marriage, Rick and Denise have always said to each other, "*Jesus is in the middle of us*. It's not just you and me — it's you and me *and Jesus*." Rick shared:

> I can truly say that God called us together because we were not in pursuit of each other. I wasn't in pursuit of anybody *except Jesus*. And Jesus revealed to me that Denise was to be both my wife and my partner in ministry. From the very beginning, God has had a purpose for our lives. And from the day we said, 'I do,' *we have been focused on what God has called us to do.*

Denise shared her insights as well, saying:

> I know there will be a lot of people in Heaven because of how God has blessed this team. There's a chemistry that God puts together, and then God's anointing comes on that couple. When you're united, there's so much you can do and so much He can do through you.

The devil is against you being united with your spouse. He wants to pull you apart and make sure that you never find your purpose as a married couple. But when you find the purpose in your marriage, it gives both of you spiritual power to stand against the enemy, and there's a good reward for your labor together.

Growing Together Over the Years Is the Blessing of God for Married Couples

In 2025, at the time of this teaching, Rick and Denise celebrate 44 years of marriage, so in this series about how to have a happy marriage, they decided to share how their marriage began and how it evolved with the Lord's guidance. In the first few years, they never had a word of strife and were as joyful as could be in the ministry together.

As you'll discover in the next lessons, eventually life situations arose, and they had to learn to work through their emotions. They had to learn how to be nice to each other, which is a part of the process of growing together in marriage. (Learn more about their amazing story in their autobiography, *Unlikely.*) Their marriage has been quite unlikely, but God loves to do unlikely things. When He is in the center of our lives — including our marriage — He helps us live out our purpose for His glory!

STUDY QUESTIONS

Study to shew thyself approved unto God, a workman that needeth not to be ashamed, rightly dividing the word of truth.
— 2 Timothy 2:15

1. In the program, Denise shared that many years ago, the Lord said to her, "I didn't call you to aspire to the Metropolitan Opera, but that the praises of God would come out of you, over this pipe, and give glory and honor to Me." At that moment, she received her call from the Lord, so she changed her whole summer plan although she had a fully paid scholarship to an opera camp in Europe. The Lord called her to sing His praises, and she obeyed Him.

   - What about *you*? When the Holy Spirit leads you to do something contrary to your plans, what is your response to Him?

   - What are some of the blessings of obeying His leadings? (*See* Luke 5:4-6; Genesis 22:15-18.)

   - What are some consequences for disobedience? (*See* 1 Samuel 15:23; Jonah 1:1-3, 17.)

- Is there something God asked you to do that you need to say yes to right now?

- Why wait? Say yes to His call and leading! (*See* 1 Corinthians 2:9-10; Hebrews 12:1; Acts 26:14-19.)

2. In the program, Rick shared how his original mindset was to remain single and undistracted — like the apostle Paul. Then he met Denise and soon after asked her to marry him. After the initial proposal, fear kept him from moving forward with their relationship, even after Jesus revealed to him that Denise was to be both his wife and partner in ministry. It took time, but Rick and Denise finally married. And from the day they said, "I do," they have been fulfilling God's call *together*!

- Why was it so vital for Rick to be willing to lay down his plan to remain single?

- What does the Bible say about the plan of God for your life? (*See* Jeremiah 29:11-13; Proverbs 3:5-6.)

- Why is it so important to consecrate to God's plan for your life? (*See* Psalm 127:1; Matthew 7:24-27; Isaiah 1:19.)

- Would God's perfect will for Rick's life have been accomplished if he ignored the leading of the Lord in marrying Denise?

- How can that important lesson be applied to *your* life?

PRACTICAL APPLICATION

**But be ye doers of the word, and not hearers only,
deceiving your own selves.
—James 1:22**

1. Rick mentioned that from the very beginning, God had a purpose for his life and for Denise's life as well. Likewise, God has a purpose for *your* life! And He has a purpose for your *marriage*! If you are married:

- Set aside time with your spouse to pray. (*See* Matthew 18:19 *NKJV*; Colossians 4:2 *NKJV*; 1 Timothy 2:1-2; Ephesians 6:18.)

- Ask the Lord to reveal His purpose for your marriage. (*See* Jeremiah 33:3; 1 John 5:14-15.)

- Write down what He tells you. (*See* Habakkuk 2:2-3.)

- Pray diligently over the plan of God for your marriage. (*See* Jude 20; Romans 8:26-27.)

- Cooperate with the Holy Spirit as He leads you step by step. (*See* Romans 8:14.)

2. Are you single and trusting God for a spouse? Then pursue God with all your heart. It's very possible that you have more time and less responsibilities now than you will once you get married, so savor your intimate fellowship with the Lord and focus your energy on serving Him! He will bring the right person to you at the right time. (*See* John 15:4-5; Philippians 3:9-10; Ecclesiastes 3:1.) Pray this from your heart: *Lord, I love You with all my heart, soul, mind, and strength. I want to know You and commune with You intimately every day. Reveal Yourself to me in Your Word. Show me how I can serve You and further Your Kingdom. I would like to be married someday, Lord, and I cast the care of that onto You. I thank You for bringing my spouse to me at the right time, and when You do, I'll know it. And we'll serve You together for the rest of our lives. Thank You, Lord, in Jesus' name. Amen.*

LESSON 2

TOPIC

Does Your Marriage Have Purpose?

SCRIPTURES

1. **Ecclesiastes 4:12** — And if one prevail against him, two shall withstand him; and a threefold cord is not quickly broken.

2. **Ecclesiastes 3:1–8** — To every thing there is a season, and a time to every purpose under the heaven: a time to be born, and a time to die; a time to plant, and a time to pluck up that which is planted; a time to kill, and a time to heal; a time to break down, and a time to build up; a time to weep, and a time to laugh; a time to mourn, and a time to dance; a time to cast away stones, and a time to gather stones together; a time to embrace, and a time to refrain from embracing; a time to get, and a time to lose; a time to keep, and a time to cast away; a time to rend, and a time to sew; a time to keep silence, and a time to

speak; a time to love, and a time to hate; a time of war, and a time of peace.

3. **Ecclesiastes 4:9** — Two are better than one; because they have a good reward for their labour.

4. **Proverbs 29:18** — Where there is no vision, the people perish: but he that keepeth the law, happy is he.

5. **Philippians 3:13-14** — Brethren, I count not myself to have apprehended: but this one thing I do, forgetting those things which are behind, and reaching forth unto those things which are before, I press toward the mark for the prize of the high calling of God in Christ Jesus.

GREEK WORDS

No Greek words were shown on the TV program.

SYNOPSIS

In the previous lesson, Rick and Denise shared how their marriage began and how we need to make Christ the center of our marriage. During their marriage ceremony, they committed to serving one another for the rest of their lives before God. At the time, Rick was the pastor for the single-adults group in their church, and when they married, they became the single-adult pastors together and immediately started in ministry.

Included in that group were people recovering from divorce, and Rick began to study things that build a happy marriage. One thing that caused so many of these other marriages to fail became clear. Rick noticed it seemed a lot of these failed marriages didn't have *a purpose*. When you have a purpose for your relationship, it holds you and your spouse together and gives you a goal for your life and your marriage. Proverbs 29:18 says, "Where there is no vision the people perish." That's how vital purpose is to your marriage!

The emphasis of this lesson:

Marriages that lack a purpose tend to flounder — but when you recognize that you and your spouse have a God-ordained purpose to fulfill, it empowers you for success! When your marriage has a purpose, it gives you direction, it gives you power, it gives you energy, and it gives you

something to work for. It is amazing what a purpose will do for your marriage!

Keep Jesus in the Center of Your Marriage

Unity is essential in a marriage relationship. The Bible tells us in Ecclesiastes 4:12, "And if one prevail against him, two shall withstand him...." When you are united in marriage, you and your spouse have great spiritual power to stand against the enemy.

Ecclesiastes 4:12 says, "...And a threefold cord is not quickly broken." When you make Jesus the center of your relationship, it causes your marriage to be "a threefold cord." Rick said, "From the very outset of our marriage, Denise and I said it was the two of us with Jesus in the center of our relationship. It wasn't just Denise and me — it was us and Jesus." When Jesus is at the center of your relationship, He makes your marriage strong.

In life, there are circumstances that come against us — events, disappointments, financial struggles, and all kinds of situations that the devil orchestrates to try to pull you apart from your spouse and discourage you. But when Jesus is included in your marriage, then it's not just you and your spouse — it is a "threefold cord" with Jesus in the middle. And when He is at the center, He can hold you together regardless of what comes against you.

Rick and Denise have a 44-year testimony of that. They affirmed, "We've encountered a lot of things in 44 years, but here we are and we're happy! And we're going to remain happy for the rest of our lives because Jesus is in the middle of our relationship."

Every Marriage Needs a Purpose

When Rick and Denise were first married, they served as the single adult group pastors in a large church. They also started a ministry to newly divorced people called Starting Over. Rick shared:

> When we opened the door for that ministry to begin, we did not realize what a flood we would have in terms of response. I thought maybe a few people would show up for a seminar we held. Denise and I were brand-new in our marriage, and in the

first year of our marriage, our "Starting Over" ministry had 1,100 new divorcees come through — 1,100 in just one year.

It was a cyclical seminar which would repeat, and every single time, it was jam-packed with people getting saved and being restored. But that year, at the very outset of our marriage, I began to study what caused all these other marriages to fail. And one thing I noticed is it seemed a lot of these marriages didn't have a purpose.

Friend, when you don't have a purpose bigger than yourself, then, even if you love your spouse, eventually you get frustrated in your marriage. You can begin to wonder, *Isn't there more than this?* People begin to think about other things, and they begin to drift. But when you have a purpose for your relationship, it holds you and your spouse together and gives you a goal for your life and your marriage. Then when you begin to have kids, it gives a goal and direction to your entire family.

A Purpose-Filled Marriage Has Great Reward

Everything needs a purpose, including your marriage. And *everyone* needs a purpose, as we see in Ecclesiastes 3:1–8. These verses declare:

> **To every thing there is a season, and a time to every purpose under the heaven: a time to be born, and a time to die; a time to plant, and a time to pluck up that which is planted; a time to kill, and a time to heal; a time to break down, and a time to build up; a time to weep, and a time to laugh; a time to mourn, and a time to dance; a time to cast away stones, and a time to gather stones together; a time to embrace, and a time to refrain from embracing; a time to get, and a time to lose; a time to keep, and a time to cast away; a time to rend, and a time to sew; a time to keep silence, and a time to speak; a time to love, and a time to hate; a time of war, and a time of peace.**

There is a time and a purpose for everything. Just as every person is created with a purpose, when God calls two people together, He brings them together with *divine purpose*. There's a divine chemistry which takes place.

Ecclesiastes 4:9 teaches us, "Two are better than one; because they have a good reward for their labour." You know that God has given you a call when you and your spouse are working together. When He has given you a vision and you labor together — you have an amazing result or reward!

Rick and Denise shared that when they look back on their marriage, they can see 44 years of fruitfulness because their two gifts came together. They had to learn how to make those gifts work together because each of them is gifted differently. But God showed Rick and Denise, and is still showing them, how to bring their gifts together so they can become more fruitful as a team.

Realize That Marriage Is a Sacred Covenant

It's so important to recognize that holy matrimony is *a covenant*. When you get married, it is a covenant *with God* and *with your spouse*. That covenant is the basis on which you build your God-given mission together. Friends, the purpose of your marriage is significant, but the foundation of it must be your covenant with God and with each other.

When storms come against you and your calling — and they do come — you can go back to your covenant. You can go back to the commitment you made to one another. And together, you can go through those storms. Those storms reveal what's on the inside of you and allow you to dig deeper into Christ.

Rick and Denise shared that in their marriage the word "divorce" has never been spoken. They don't allow it. When married people jokingly say to their spouse, "I'm going to divorce you," it is not funny. Ministering to divorcees taught them how tragic it is for the person, for the couple, and for their children. There is nothing funny about divorce. Eliminate that word from your vocabulary.

If you've already been through a divorce, then you know how destructive the effects of it are. But Jesus is anointed to heal the broken-hearted. If you've been broken-hearted, Jesus can heal you. He can heal any fracture your heart is dealing with and bring you to a place of wholeness again.

Recognize Your Purpose in Marriage

When Rick and Denise got married, they knew they were both called to the ministry. He didn't have his ministry alone while she had her ministry alone. They could have, but God called them *together* so there would be a blending of their ministries.

Together, their God-given mission has been to reach the world, take the teaching of the Bible to the ends of the earth, and build up the Body of Christ. They have an apostolic calling on their lives, and they have worked on the front lines *together*, preaching and pushing back darkness *together*. Rick shared, "We've done what other people said was impossible, but we've done it *together with the Lord* because He's in the middle of all of us with our family. Our purpose has been very clearly defined."

Your calling may not be working in the ministry but there are all kinds of callings. It may be to raise up godly children who have an impact on the world. It may be in the business realm. God may anoint you and your spouse to make money so you'll be blessed, and so you can fund the Gospel around the world. In the program, Rick shared, "We have a very dear couple who are our friends, and they're just anointed to make money because they believe they're called to fund the Gospel. That is their purpose. And wow! They've embraced it, and they have a good reward for their labor."

When you know your God-given purpose and embrace it, you have a good reward for what you do. Know that God didn't call you and your spouse together so you could merely sit in your house, watch TV, eat, go to bed, wake up, go to work, and do it all over again. That's what an animal does. An animal just gets up, eats, does what it does, goes back to sleep, and repeats the cycle day after day.

But there's more to life than that. Whether you're single or married, you are born to be more than an animal. Your life is designed to be more impactful than that! And when God calls you to somebody in marriage, there needs to be a purpose to that union. One reason people struggle in their marriages is that they don't have a vision to give themselves to, so they become frustrated and dissatisfied. But when you have a mission, when you have a goal, when you know why you're here, when you know why your marriage has been formed by the Lord — it puts everything on a different level.

The Powerful Purpose of a Woman in Marriage

The woman's role in marriage is powerful. Marriage doesn't diminish her talents or gifts in any way. But in the home, women are particularly powerful because the Bible says that she was made for man (*see* 1 Corinthians 11:9).

Men need women, and in fact, the woman is the glory of her husband (*see* 1 Corinthians 11:7).

Men *need* a woman's support. Ladies, your husband needs your good words and consistency. Husbands need their wives to love, nurture, and help take care of the children and the house. Part of a woman's purpose in marriage is taking that place of responsibility in the home.

Rather than embracing this role and enjoying the season of raising and nurturing their children, so many mothers just hurriedly wait for their children to grow up. Then these same mothers worry about what will happen to their grown, adult children who have left the house. We need to *enjoy* each season that God has given us and embrace it — not just wish that time would go away when our children are young. Those are precious years, and raising our children to know and walk with God is part of our purpose as parents, in which women play a vital role. Women are so powerful!

The Apostle Peter's Insights Into Marriage

In First Peter 3, Peter addressed the subject of marriage. Peter was married for about 60 years, so when he wrote about marriage, he was speaking from a wealth of life experiences. We know that Peter's wife traveled with him in the ministry, and for a wife to willingly travel everywhere with a suitcase, she must be a happy person. So Peter had a very happy marriage, and he and his wife were together all the way to the end. Their story is quite amazing.

When Peter addresses husbands and wives, he addresses them in seven verses. The first six verses are written to wives and show how much power a wife has. Part of the purpose for a wife in a marriage is to find out what she is to be like to thrive in that role, how she is to serve, and what she is to do regarding their children. In First Peter 3:1–6, there is amazing guidance and direction for wives to glean from.

In verse 7, Peter spoke very briefly to men. He was straight with the men and gave amazing direction to them, saying that husbands and wives are called together that they might be inheritors of the grace of life. Marriage is supposed to be a partnership that brings forth great fruit.

In fact, verse 7 even says that when you walk in unity together, your prayers won't be hindered. The devil will not have the ability to disrupt your prayers when you're walking in unity with your spouse in your marriage. A couple that is united has great power in prayer.

Every Marriage Needs a Vision

We all need a vision for our lives. According to Proverbs 29:18, "Where there is no vision, the people perish...." Likewise, when marriages don't have a vision or a purpose, those relationships begin to flounder and eventually perish. But in Philippians 3:13, the apostle Paul talked about his own life and gave us a principle that also applies to marriage. He wrote, "Brethren, I count not myself to have apprehended...."

The phrase "count not" is a bookkeeping term. It is the picture of a bookkeeper who has a ledger in front of him. On one page, he has all the original projections, the goal, or the vision, but on the other side of the page, he has the actual numbers. The bookkeeper looks at the original projections, the goal, the vision, and then he looks on the other side of the page to consider the real numbers and see how well they match up.

Paul said, in essence, "Brethren, when I look at my life and when I look at what God called me to do, the vision and purpose for my life is very clear. But when I look at the reality of what I've accomplished, I count not myself to have apprehended the goal. I see that the numbers don't match the vision. I've done a lot, but I haven't done everything God has called me to do." The only way that Paul knew he hadn't fulfilled it all was because he had a vision to adhere to. He knew what he was supposed to do.

Every person and every marriage needs a vision. Focusing on your purpose gives you drive and energy. It gives you something to pray about, and it gives you the ability to know where you are in your life. Are you doing what God has called you to do? How far have you come along in fulfilling what He has called you and your spouse to accomplish?

Reach for the Fullness of God's Vision for Your Marriage

Paul went on to say in Philippians 3:13 and 14, "...but this one thing I do, forgetting those things which are behind, and reaching forth unto those things which are before, I press toward the mark for the prize of the high calling of God in Christ Jesus." In this verse, we are admonished to leave the past behind and press toward the "mark for the prize of the high calling of God in Christ Jesus."

Philippians 3:13 and 14 applies to you personally, as an individual, but it also applies to your marriage. You and your spouse can look at each other and say, "We're not done yet." How do you know you're not done? It's because you know the vision. You know what God has called you to do. And when you look at what you've done and compare it to what God has told you to do, you can tell you still have some work to do. The vision is not completed yet, so it's not time for you to sit on the couch and retire. You have a purpose. And you can choose to live out your purpose to the very end.

The apostle Paul said, "I press forward." You must do this because there will be opposition against your calling. You have to press forward and embrace what God has put in your heart to do as an individual and as a couple. You are to embrace the commitment you have to pray for your children and what you need to do for your kids — and act on it. Success doesn't happen by accident.

Seek God To Find Your Purpose as a Couple

Every person has an individual calling, and when two people come together in holy matrimony, then they have a purpose to accomplish as a married couple. They bring together their two callings and good fruit is produced. According to Ecclesiastes 4:9, "Two are better than one; because they have a good reward for their labour."

Friend, there is a reason for your life and God has an assignment for you — you simply need to wake up to it. And you must have a vision for your marriage as well. It would be good for you and your spouse to pray together and ask what your marriage is for. Is it just about the two of you? Or is there something bigger than yourselves that God wants you to achieve with your marriage?

Remember, when your marriage has a purpose, it gives you direction. Focusing on your direction as a couple gives you power and energy. It gives you something to work toward. It is amazing what a vision will do for your marriage. If you are ready to take that step, here's how you can pray:

Father, we pray right now in the name of Jesus to have spiritual ears to hear what the Spirit has to say to us about the purpose of our marriage. Holy Spirit, give us the vision for what You want our lives to accomplish. Give us a goal and help us to rally around it. In Jesus' name. Amen.

STUDY QUESTIONS

Study to shew thyself approved unto God, a workman that needeth not to be ashamed, rightly dividing the word of truth.
— 2 Timothy 2:15

1. Did you know there are prayers in the Bible that you can pray daily to help you discover and fulfill your purpose? (*See* Ephesians 1:16-23; Ephesians 3:14-21; Colossians 1:9-15.)

2. According to Ecclesiastes 4:9, "Two are better than one; because they have a good reward for their labour." Have you ever considered the fact that you and your spouse will be *rewarded* for obeying God and following His purpose for your life? That's something to look forward to! Will it be worth it? What does the Bible have to say about the blessing of finishing your purpose-filled race? (*See* 2 Timothy 4:7-8; Colossians 3:23-24.)

3. You have a divine purpose as a married couple. Realize there will be opposition against that calling, and to finish your God-given assignment, you'll need to make an unwavering decision to "press toward the mark for the prize of the high calling of God in Christ Jesus" (Philippians 3:13-14). Have you armed yourself with scriptures to stand on when the enemy tries to thwart your progress? Here are some powerful verses to get you started. (*See* 1 John 4:4; Isaiah 54:17; Joshua 24:15; 1 Corinthians 15:57-58.)

PRACTICAL APPLICATION

But be ye doers of the word, and not hearers only, deceiving your own selves.
— James 1:22

1. In the program, Rick and Denise shared that in their marriage the word "divorce" has never been spoken. They don't allow it. What about you? Have you and your spouse eliminated the word "divorce" from your marriage? Take time now to be honest with God if you have allowed yourselves to bring up the weighty subject of divorce in

reference to your relationship. Words are powerful! Ask God and your spouse for forgiveness and commit yourselves to keeping "divorce" out of your vocabulary. An exception to this is if you or your children are in danger or are being physically or emotionally harmed by your spouse. If that is the case, contact a counselor, pastor, or a domestic-violence hotline for help in developing a safety plan.

2.   Marriage is a partnership with the potential to bring forth great fruit. First Peter 3:7 even says, "…Being heirs together of the grace of life; that your prayers be not hindered." When you and your spouse walk in unity, *your prayers won't be hindered!* Wow! The devil will not have the ability to disrupt your prayers when you're walking as "heirs together of the grace of life." Think about the massive consequences of allowing anything to bring division or strife into your marriage. (*See* James 3:16; Proverbs 6:16,19.) Make the decision ahead of time that if you become tempted to get out of unity with your spouse, you will resist the temptation and yield to the love of God instead. (*See* James 4:7; Romans 5:5.)

3.   A practical thing you can do in your marriage to maintain unity is to read First Corinthians 13:4-8 (*AMPC*) out loud every day. Put your name in these verses and personalize them. Why? Because the Bible instructs us to "…put on love, which is the perfect bond of unity" (Colossians 3:14 *NASB*). If you let the love of God flow through you to your spouse, you'll stay in the place of unity and your prayers will not be hindered. Instead, they will be abundantly fruitful! (*See* John 15:7-8; John 13:34-35; and James 5:16 *AMPC*.)

<hr>

LESSON 3

TOPIC
Can You Shut the Door to Strife?

SCRIPTURES
1.   **Ephesians 4:27** — Neither give place to the devil.
2.   **James 3:16** — For where envying and strife is, there is confusion and every evil work.

3. **1 Peter 3:9** — Not rendering evil for evil, or railing for railing: but contrariwise blessing; knowing that ye are thereunto called, that ye should inherit a blessing.

4. **1 Peter 3:9** (*RIV*) — You absolutely must not try to get even, get revenge, or pay someone back for what he or she did to you or to someone else. Don't try to settle the score by repaying someone for his or her bad, evil, malicious, rotten attitudes and behavior by exchanging bad, evil, malicious, rotten attitudes and behavior. If someone has verbally abused, berated, damaged, debased, harassed, humiliated, insulted, or misused you or someone else, do not make it your business to pay him or her back with the same kind of verbal abuse. But — on the contrary — that is, on the farthest, opposite end of the spectrum, you must instead speak a blessing in response to that person. For it is for this very purpose that you have been prestigiously called — that you should be the recipients of blessing.

5. **Proverbs 15:1** — A soft answer turneth away wrath: but grievous words stir up anger.

6. **Ecclesiastes 3:7** — ...A time to keep silence, and a time to speak.

7. **Ecclesiastes 3:5** — ...A time to embrace, and a time to refrain from embracing.

8. **1 Peter 5:8** — Be sober, be vigilant; because your adversary the devil, as a roaring lion, walketh about, seeking whom he may devour.

GREEK WORDS

1. "place" — **τόπος** (*topos*): a real geographical location; a door, window, or crack

2. "evil" — **φαῦλος** (*phaulos*): foul things

3. "evil" — **κακός** (*kakos*): describes bad, evil, malicious, or rotten attitudes and behaviors

4. "for" — **ἀντί** (*anti*): in exchange for

SYNOPSIS

Along the road of life, there are a lot of bumps. But you can get past the road bumps and walk in peace. You can walk in the Spirit and have a happy marriage like Rick and Denise enjoy. This lesson shares what they have learned about shutting the door to strife in their lives. And it is important that every one of us does this. Strife opens the door to every evil thing, including sickness and even accidents. We can avoid the evil things the devil plans for us when we choose to refuse strife and to walk in God's peace toward our spouse and family.

The emphasis of this lesson:

God brings unity into a marriage when He is at the center, and it becomes a place of peace and purpose. The devil will try to bring strife into the relationship to disrupt that unity; however, you have the power — through the Holy Spirit within you — to *resist* strife. In fact, it is wise to implement a "no strife" policy in your marriage — and choose to *bless* one another instead.

Strife Opens a Door to the Enemy

Soon after Rick and Denise were married, they found themselves traveling across the United States in a tiny little Isuzu automobile at the start of their traveling teaching ministry. As Rick and Denise began ministering throughout the nation, the Lord gave him a vision. Rick shared:

> I saw a ring of fire burning around the perimeter of the United States, and the Lord said to me, 'Follow the fire.' So that's what Denise and I did. We drove north through the central part of the United States to Minnesota. Then we turned west and drove across Montana, Idaho, Washington state, Oregon, and California. We came down into Arizona and New Mexico, making a circle around the United States. And then we came inward to the center part of the States again.

> As Denise and I traveled, our son Paul was in the backseat and he was two years old. Our other son, Philip, had just been born and was six weeks old. Sometimes it got a little tense in our car because Paul never wanted to stay in the car seat. We had to keep putting him back in his car seat over and over. It was so bad that I would pull the car over, get out, and put Paul back in his seat. By the time I was back in the driver's seat, Paul was already out again. He just refused to stay there.

> We drove down the road with Philip on Denise's lap, crying. Paul was in the backseat, refusing to stay in the car seat. We were so close to each other that Denise and I were nearly joined at the hip. The floorboard was covered with things and our luggage

was packed on top of the car. We looked like the leaning Tower of Pisa. We carried a tape duplicator in the trunk, along with a typewriter, plus luggage. It was pretty tight and these trips were typically two months long.

Our ministry was just starting out. We were young and didn't have much money. I was believing God for the gas money for every mile we traveled and money to pay for all the hotels and do all the ministry. The responsibility was just all so huge. And it got a little tense in the car because Paul was not in the car seat and Philip was crying. Every once in a while, Denise and I — who really loved each other — would get tense, and it was like a spirit of strife would come between us.

Denise and I are not strife-filled people. That's just not who we are. We are peace-loving people. But whenever we would get into strife, one of our sons would get sick. Finally, we woke up one day and realized that every time we got into strife, one of the kids got sick. And we began to understand that strife was a door for the enemy to get in.

Saying No to Strife Is Crucial

How do we close the door to strife in our lives? Ephesians 4:27 instructs, "Neither give place to the devil." The word "place" in Greek is the word *topos*. It describes *a real geographical location; a door, window, or crack*. It's a location that is just as real as any physical door, window, or crack. When Rick and Denise got into strife with each other, it opened a door and gave place to the devil, and their children would get sick. One day, an awful event took place. Rick said:

In a moment of strife between me and Denise, our infant son Philip reached over and accidentally put his hand into a cup of piping hot coffee — and it melted all the skin off his hand. In the middle of our travels, Denise and I had to take Philip to the hospital every single day. Everywhere we went, the first thing we had to do was locate the emergency room because every day they had to cut off dead skin and treat his hand. They had to tend to it day after day after day. Every time we went to have Philip's hand treated, I was reminded that the burn on it took place during a moment of strife.

James 3:16 teaches us, "For where envying and strife is, there is confusion and every evil work." The word "evil" here is the Greek word *phaulos*, which describes *foul things*. As a result of their experience with their son, Rick said:

> Denise and I made a decision that we were going to have a 'no strife' policy. You may say, 'Have you really lived by that?' Actually, we have. There have been very few moments in our 44 years of marriage and ministry that we've had strife.

Negative Emotions Are Within Your Control

So how do you keep strife from entering your marriage or home? Friends, it is a *decision*. Strife is an emotion. An important statement to remember is this: *Emotions are expensive, and you have to decide how you're going to spend them.* If you choose to spend your emotions on strife, it will open the door for bad things.

You can choose to reserve your emotions for something positive. Emotions are within your control, and the devil works through emotions that have not been brought under control. This is how strife enters in. However, you can control yourself, and you can control strife. How do you know this is true?

Consider what usually happens when you and your spouse are fighting with each other, and suddenly the phone rings. In most cases you change your behavior immediately and say, "Hello! I'm doing great. How are you?" You're not doing great at all, but you're able to pull yourself together because you choose to. Rick explained:

> When our kids were growing up, they didn't see strife in our home because we had a 'no strife' policy. Now that does not mean we didn't have the opportunity for strife. *Strife is a spirit.* You can feel it when strife comes. It tempts you. It lures you in, but you have to say no to it. And friend, if you make no room for it, then you won't get into strife.
>
> If Denise and I were tempted to get into strife, sometimes we would say, 'I need a few minutes by myself.' We'd go to another place alone or take a walk or do something to get away, calm ourselves down, and get our emotions under control — because

we learned that when you get into strife, you open the door for bad things to take place.

This decision was so powerful in the lives of Rick and Denise that they carried the policy into their ministry as well. Within a ministry that is large and has a lot of employees, there are opportunities for people to have disagreements. There is nothing wrong with disagreeing, but *the way you deal with it is very important*. Strife is never helpful. It always opens the door for the devil. So even in their ministry and churches, Rick and Denise have a "no strife" policy.

When you have a "no strife" policy, people don't get into strife. It doesn't happen simply because you don't open the door for it. Living and working this way requires people to pray. It requires people to grow up and discuss things maturely. You can choose not to allow strife into your marriage relationship and with your children, even in communicating with your adult children, because strife opens a door for every evil work.

Look at Strife for What It Is

James 3:16 (*NKJV*) says, "For where envy and self-seeking exist, confusion and every evil thing are there." Strife results from a mindset of self-seeking and focusing on how important you are and your rights and boundaries. It comes from an attitude that says, "I'm going to hold my line and show you I'm right and you are wrong." This way of thinking opens the door for strife to come in. And who wants confusion or every evil thing in their life?

Friend, look at strife for what it is — an emotion that brings destruction. And sometimes strife takes place when you get involved in a conversation and begin talking back and forth. First Peter 3:9 calls it "railing for railing." In this book, Peter addressed all relationships, including the one between husbands and wives.

First Peter 3:9 says, "Not rendering evil for evil, or railing for railing: but contrariwise blessing; knowing that ye are thereunto called, that ye should inherit a blessing." We're instructed not to render "evil for evil." The word "evil" is a form of the Greek word *kakos*, which describes *bad, evil, malicious, rotten attitudes and behaviors*. And when this verse says, "for evil," the word "for" is the Greek word *anti*, which means *in exchange for*. If you put all this together, you get the *Renner Interpretive Version* (*RIV*) of this verse which says, "You absolutely must not try to get even, get revenge, or pay someone back for what he or she did to you or to someone else."

How To Respond When You Are Tempted To Enter Into Strife

Consider the times in marriage that people are supposed to be listening to their spouse as he or she is talking, but they are already thinking about how they're going to respond to what that person is saying. They are not listening because they're contemplating how they're going to respond to their spouse's statement. When we take into account the original Greek meaning of the key words in this verse, the *Renner Interpretive Version* (*RIV*) of First Peter 3:9 says:

> **You absolutely must not try to get even, get revenge, or pay someone back for what he or she did to you or to someone else. Don't try to settle the score by repaying someone for his or her bad, evil, malicious, rotten attitudes and behavior by exchanging bad, evil, malicious, rotten attitudes and behavior. If someone has verbally abused, berated, damaged, debased, harassed, humiliated, insulted, or misused you or someone else, do not make it your business to pay him or her back with the same kind of verbal abuse.**

If we stopped right there, that admonishment would be enough to ponder and work on for a long time. But Peter went on to say, "…but contrariwise blessing; knowing that ye are thereunto called, that ye should inherit a blessing." The *Renner Interpretive Version* (*RIV*) of First Peter 3:9 continues on to say:

> **But — on the contrary — that is, on the farthest, opposite end of the spectrum, you must instead speak a blessing in response to that person. For it is for this very purpose that you have been prestigiously called — that you should be the recipients of blessing.**

God wants your marriage partner to be the recipient of a *blessing*. If Rick and Denise are ever tempted to get into strife, they intentionally say to each other, "You're such a blessing to me. I love you." They *make a decision* contrariwise to speak a blessing. Peter doesn't say to *think* a blessing. He says to *speak* a blessing. Blessings have to be verbalized.

You must choose not to pay each other back with negative words. Don't respond to your spouse by saying, "I know how I'm going to answer that. If that's what *you* think, just wait until you're quiet. I'm going to tell you what *I* think about that." No! Rather than getting into a dragged out, prolonged conversation that's not going to take you anywhere positive, put on the brakes, take a deep breath, and choose your words carefully.

You Are Called To Maintain Peace in Your Home

On the inside of your spirit there's a calling to bless others that comes from the spirit of love within your heart. Romans 5:5 says that when we are born again, "The love of God is shed abroad in our hearts by the Holy Ghost." From *that* place we have the power to look at our spouse if they say something offensive and respond, "I love you. You're such a blessing to me."

Gentle words can do a lot. The Bible tells us in Proverbs 15:1, "A soft answer turneth away wrath: but grievous words stir up anger." What's a soft answer? A soft answer comes from a soft place in your heart, not a hard place — not a place that declares, "I'm going to pay you back," but a place that responds, "I'm going to *bless* you."

Endeavor to learn when to speak and when to be silent. Ecclesiastes 3:7 instructs us that there is "…a time to keep silence, and a time to speak." Ecclesiastes 3:5 says there is "…a time to embrace, and a time to refrain from embracing." Sometimes when you're tempted to get into strife, it's okay to say, "This is a time for us to be quiet. This is a time for us to refrain from embracing. We need a little distance from each other to calm down."

Do whatever you have to do to maintain peace in your home, because when you open a door to the devil, he comes in. First Peter 5:8 admonishes, "Be sober, be vigilant; because your adversary the devil, as a roaring lion, walketh about, seeking whom he may devour." One of the entryways the enemy uses to find access into your life is through strife. That's often when accidents happen. That's when people get sick or things begin to go haywire. If you really reflect on it and think about it, very often *bad things happen around an event of strife.*

If you seem to be dealing with a lot of strife in your relationships, find some time alone and seek the Lord about it. Strife comes from self-seeking, and God will show you what's inside of you that causes you to be resentful and intent on getting your own way. James 3:16 (*NKJV*) says: "For where envy and self-seeking exist, confusion and every evil thing are there." Why are we so self-seeking? The root of it is fear. But God has given us His love — and from that love on the inside, we are called to bless one another and to inherit a blessing in return.

Give Your Spouse *Grace*

When you're tempted to say something unkind that will get both of you into strife, remember that you are talking with the person God has called you to unite with. You are conversing with a person who has forgiven you for many things and overlooked a lot of things. Maybe this is a moment for you to give them grace in return. Friend, forgiveness has great power in marriage.

Perhaps you are reading this while you are in a place of strife with your spouse or even contemplating divorce. Right now, the Holy Spirit is there upon both of you to recognize the union that you have together and the covenant you made before God and with each other. Your marriage is not something to throw away — it is precious, so use this moment to reevaluate what you're thinking. Come together again and recognize the good things in one another.

Why not implement a "no strife" policy in your home beginning today? If you're ready to say no to strife, pray this:

> *Father, I thank You in the name of Jesus that You've given me the power to say 'no' to a spirit of strife. And right now, I make a decision to have a 'no strife' policy in my life and in our home. I thank you that the Holy Spirit empowered me to make this decision, and He'll help me fulfill it. Thank You, Holy Spirit, for teaching me how to discuss things maturely without a spirit of strife. In Jesus' name. Amen.*

STUDY QUESTIONS

> **Study to shew thyself approved unto God, a workman that needeth not to be ashamed, rightly dividing the word of truth.**
> **— 2 Timothy 2:15**

1. Ephesians 4:27 instructs us clearly, "Neither give place to the devil." When you give place to the devil in your life, it often results in strife. And when strife gets in, every evil work is present (*see* James 3:16). Take an honest look at yourself and your marriage.

- Do you get into strife with others? What happens when you yield to strife instead of resisting it?

- What does the Bible say you should do when tempted in this area? (*See* James 4:7; 1 Peter 5:8-9.)

- Is it possible to overcome the temptation to get into strife and choose not to allow it into your marriage? (*See* Romans 8:37; 1 Corinthians 15:57.)

2. Look at strife for what it is. It opens the door to the devil and brings destruction. According to John 10:10, what does "the thief," the devil, come to do? If we open the door to strife, who are we inviting into our situation? Does that make you absolutely want to keep strife out of your marriage and home?

3. In the program, Denise mentioned that we're to recognize the good things in one another. What does the Bible teach us along these lines? (*See* Philippians 2:3-4; Proverbs 31:11-12, 28-31; 1 Corinthians 13:7 *AMPC*.)

PRACTICAL APPLICATION

**But be ye doers of the word, and not hearers only,
deceiving your own selves.
—James 1:22**

1. Rick and Denise shared a story about how their infant son accidentally put his hand into a cup of hot coffee and experienced third-degree burns as a result. This took place during a moment of strife in their marriage. In what ways can you identify with this story? Have you or your children experienced something terrible because of an atmosphere of strife that was present? What did you learn from that experience?

2. In this lesson, Rick and Denise gave the following practical advice on how to keep strife from entering your marriage or home:

- You can feel it when strife comes. It is a spirit that tempts you. It lures you in, but you have to **say no to it.** If you **make no room for it,** you won't get into strife.

- If you are tempted to get into strife, say to your spouse, "I need a few minutes by myself." **Go to someplace alone,** take a walk, calm yourself down, and **get your emotions under control.**

- Choose not to pay each other back. Rather than getting into a dragged-out conversation that's not going to take you anywhere positive, **put on the brakes and think carefully about what you are going to say before you say it.**

- It is a decision. You can control yourself and **decide to change** your behavior (just like you do when answering the phone in the middle of a tense moment — you might feel uptight, but the minute you answer the phone, your voice softens).

Reflect on these practical tips and allow them to bring positive changes to difficult situations. Ask the Holy Spirit to help you implement these when strife tries to enter your relationship with your spouse or other people in your life.

3. Take time to reread the entirety of First Peter 3:9 in the *Renner Interpretive Version* (*RIV*). What is the Holy Spirit showing you in these verses? Are there any specific adjustments you perceive He is asking you to make to be a "doer" of this passage of Scripture? Notice that Peter doesn't say to *think* a blessing. He says to *speak* a blessing. Blessings must be verbalized. What are some blessings you can speak to your spouse, particularly if you are tempted to yield to strife?

LESSON 4

TOPIC

How Important Is Grace to Marriage

SCRIPTURES

1. **Ephesians 4:27** — Neither give place to the devil.

2. **Ephesians 4:29** — Let no corrupt communication proceed out of your mouth, but that which is good to the use of edifying, that it may minister grace unto the hearers.

3. **Ephesians 4:30** — And grieve not the holy Spirit of God, whereby ye are sealed unto the day of redemption.

4. **Ephesians 4:31-32** — Let all bitterness, and wrath, and anger, and clamour, and evil speaking, be put away from you, with all malice: and

be ye kind one to another, tenderhearted, forgiving one another, even as God for Christ's sake hath forgiven you.

5. **Proverbs 16:21** — …The sweetness of the lips increaseth learning.

6. **1 Peter 3:8** — Finally, be ye all of one mind, having compassion one of another, love as brethren, be pitiful, be courteous.

7. **1 Peter 3:8** (*RIV*) — But I have a really important additional, final word. Corporately, all of you are to be synchronized as much as possible in your minds, perceptions, and understanding. You must also be compassionate, sympathetic, and empathetic toward each other, loving each other as those who are actually related to each other — in other words, love like real brothers. You must have emotions for each other so deeply felt that it moves you from a gut level to reach out to do whatever you can to help each other. Be unassuming, unpretentious, having no airs about you. Even if you're more gifted than others, don't be self-promoting, but intentionally think modestly of yourself.

8. **1 Peter 3:9** — Not rendering evil for evil, or railing for railing….

9. **1 Corinthians 12:13** — …Have been all made to drink into one Spirit.

10. **1 Peter 3:9** (*RIV*) — You absolutely must not try to get even, get revenge, or pay someone back for what he or she did to you or to someone else. Don't try to settle the score by repaying someone for his or her bad, evil, malicious, rotten attitudes and behavior by exchanging bad, evil, malicious, rotten attitudes and behavior. If someone has verbally abused, berated, damaged, debased, harassed, humiliated, insulted, or misused you or someone else, do not make it your business to pay him or her back with the same kind of verbal abuse. But — on the contrary — that is, on the farthest, opposite end of the spectrum, you must instead speak a blessing in response to that person. For it is for this very purpose that you have been prestigiously called — that you should be the recipients of blessing.

11. **1 Peter 3:10** — For he that will love life, and see good days, let him refrain his tongue from evil, and his lips that they speak no guile.

12. **1 Peter 3:10** (*RIV*) — For the person who fully intends to have a life that is full of gusto and zest — that is, a life really worth having and loving — and who wishes to see and personally experience really good and profitable days, times, and seasons in life, let him make sure his tongue refrains and ceases from speaking evil — [if a person wants to have a life filled with gusto and zest — a life really worth having and

loving — that is, blessed] — he must purposely put distance between himself and evil. And that includes watching what he says, no longer allowing his mouth to spue [reckless words] or to converse in such a way that baits others and drags them into negative conversations.

GREEK WORDS

1. "place" — τόπος (*topos*): a real geographical location; a door, window, or crack
2. "corrupt" — σαπρός (*sapros*): anything that is rotting
3. "be ye" — γίνομαι (*ginomai*): to become; the process of becoming kind to one another
4. "forgiving" — χαριζόμενοι (*charidzomenoi*): would be better translated as gracing one another

SYNOPSIS

We have seen that strife can cause great destruction to a marriage and open the door to all manner of evil things in our lives. The remedy for this is walking in forgiveness and grace. In the same way that we desire grace when *we* have made mistakes, often the best thing we can do for our spouse is to extend grace to him or her. Offering grace to one another is especially vital, as we are all brothers and sisters in the Lord, and we are to love one another as He has loved us.

The emphasis of this lesson:

As husbands and wives, we are called to give grace to each other as God for Christ's sake has given grace to us. As we learn to see our spouse as God's beloved child — as our brother or sister in Christ — we can bring His kindness, forgiveness, and love into our marriage.

You Can Keep Grace and Peace In Your Marriage — and Keep Strife OUT!

In this lesson, we look at embracing forgiveness in the context of marriage. If you want to have a happy marriage, then you have to learn how to forgive — and forgive very quickly. Ephesians 4:27 instructs us clearly, "Neither give place to the devil." In our previous lesson, we said that when you give place to the devil, it often results in strife. And when strife gets into an area, every evil work is also present (*see* James 3:16).

Early on in Rick and Denise's marriage, they learned that when strife came in, their children would get sick. It took a while to recognize the pattern, but they eventually realized there was a connection between an atmosphere of strife and their children's health. Their infant son, Philip, put his hand in hot coffee while Rick and Denise were in strife with each other and got third-degree burns on his hand. Strife opened the door for that accident to occur.

One day as they were traveling in the car and strife arose between them, Rick told Denise, "If we allow this to continue, something's going to happen." They had finally learned that strife opened a door to every evil work, and they responded by refusing to give it a place in their relationship. Rick said, "We literally rolled down the window on both sides of the car and we said, 'Strife, get out of this car!'"

Strife is a spirit sent by the devil. And when you allow it in, it creates bad things. Rick and Denise developed a "no strife" policy in their home. Ephesians 4:27 instructs us clearly, "Neither give place to the devil." The word "place" is the Greek word *topos*. It describes *a real geographical location*; *a door, window, or crack*. The devil looks for a way to get in, so you must be sure that you give him no place.

Communicate That Which Uplifts Another, and Make Your Words a Blessing

It's important to choose your words with care. In Ephesians 4:29, the Bible declares, "Let no corrupt communication proceed out of your mouth...." You may have thought this verse is speaking about curse words, but the word "corrupt" is the Greek word *sapros*, which describes *anything that is rotting*. You don't have to use curse words to speak corrupt communication, because corrupt communication is anything that produces rot. It doesn't produce anything that's good — it just produces rot because it is corrupt.

This verse goes on to explain, "Let no corrupt communication proceed out of your mouth, but that which is good to the use of edifying, that it may minister grace unto the hearers." Friends, sometimes we need to stop and ask ourselves, *Is there a benefit to what I'm saying to my spouse? Am I going to take my spouse higher or lower?*

We may need to find a different way to re-present our argument or what we are trying to say. It may benefit us to repackage our words to make them a blessing, rather than something that is corrupt and produces something bad.

Do Not Grieve the Holy Spirit —
Show Grace to Others Instead

The Bible continues to instruct us in how to communicate in Ephesians 4:30, which says, "And grieve not the holy Spirit of God, whereby ye are sealed unto the day of redemption." At times, we may need to stop and consider whether our communication is blessing the Spirit of God, or whether it is grievous to Him. You'll know the answer.

If the way you behave or speak is grieving the Holy Spirit, then you ought to stop it. If it grieves the Holy Spirit, it will grieve your spouse and it will grieve you too. Later on, you will be sorry that you talked like that. Friend, you have to do this *on purpose*. It is an intentional choice. Communicating this way doesn't happen accidentally. You must do this on purpose.

The following verses, Ephesians 4:31 and 32, declare, "Let all bitterness, and wrath, and anger, and clamour, and evil speaking, be put away from you, with all malice: and be ye kind one to another, tenderhearted, forgiving one another, even as God for Christ's sake hath forgiven you." If we can simply be nice in our communications with others, it is a sign we are a mature Christian. Simply being nice can be impressive, but it is a decision. We *choose* to be nice.

Become a Source of Grace and
Kindness to Your Spouse

Rather than spending all of your emotions on bitterness, wrath, anger, clamor, and evil speaking, put it away from you, along with all malice. Instead, as the Scripture says, "…be ye kind one to another." The word "be" is a form of the Greek word *ginomai*, which means *to become*. A better translation of "be ye kind" would be to *be in the process of becoming kind one to another* — which means this is something you have to learn.

You must learn how to put on the brakes and reverse what you said or did. You must get involved in the process of becoming "…kind one to another, tenderhearted and forgiving one another, even as God for Christ's sake hath forgiven you" (Ephesians 4:32). The word "forgiving" here is the Greek word *charidzomenoi*, which would be better translated as *gracing one another* as God for Christ's sake hath *graced* you.

How many times have you thought, *I wish my spouse would give me grace in this situation.* In the same way you want somebody to grace you, sometimes the best thing you can do is to grace somebody else. Just let it go. You don't have to correct every single thing that happens. You may want to teach and put things in order, but sometimes teaching is not the answer.

At times, the best choice is to overlook it, let it go, and extend grace to somebody in their situation. Grace the other person just as you want to be graced when you make a mistake. When you grace somebody and love him or her in spite of what happened, it is powerful. It frees people to hear from God and frees them to decide to change on their own.

Be Tenderhearted and Forgive
as Christ Has Forgiven You

Proverbs 16:21 advises, "…The sweetness of the lips increaseth learning." There is learning in sweet talk. If people are arguing or shouting at each other, then nobody hears anything, and no learning can go on. But Ephesians 4:32 instructs us to be *tenderhearted*.

When your spouse rails against you, friend, what are you to do? Should you decide to bitterly guard your heart against him or her so that person cannot hurt you? Do you think only about how to sharply answer your spouse in response? That is not a tender heart — that's a hard heart. God didn't create marriage for us to be hardhearted toward each other. That is not how marriage is supposed to be.

Rather, God has called us to be *tenderhearted* toward each other. Marriage is to be filled with understanding, supportive behavior — giving grace to one another and keeping a tender heart toward our spouse. As husbands and wives, we are to grace each other as God for Christ's sake has graced us. Think of how God has graced us. How can we be judgmental of anybody else, when we think about how nonjudgmental God has been of us? He has graced us and graced us. Friend, as believers we are obligated to grace others in the same way.

We are to forgive as we've been forgiven. Again, Ephesians 4:32 admonishes us, "…forgiving one another, even as God for Christ's sake hath forgiven you." That's a high standard. We may say, "I don't want to forgive that person anymore. I'm tired of their actions. They always do this or that and we never get along." But we must press through. And sometimes, pressing through means that we *back off and give grace.*

Intentionally think a good thought about that person you are frustrated with. Think of a good attribute about your spouse. Decide that you will be thankful for them instead of unthankful and call to remembrance good things about who they are and your relationship with them. The enemy comes in with accusations, because he is an accuser. He will either accuse you, or he will accuse your spouse through thoughts in your mind. This is why you must decide that you will keep a tender heart.

Determine To Be of One Mind With Your Spouse

The apostle Peter was married for about 60 years, and he knew something about marriage. When most people read First Peter 3, they think his speech about marriage ends in verse 7. But he continued in verse 8, which instructs, "Finally, be ye all of one mind, having compassion one of another, love as brethren, be pitiful, be courteous."

This verse is really helpful in our relationships. It admonishes us to "be ye all of one mind." The goal is to be of "one mind" with each other, so we are to have compassion toward one another. In the context of marriage, sometimes you need to have compassion in a situation. There are times when your spouse doesn't need your words, but a hug instead. We need to be reminded that sometimes people don't need correction. They need a hug to help them and a hug can fix a lot of things.

In the program, Denise gave practical advice to women. She mentioned that, at times, we may expect our husband to read our mind. We think that he knows how we feel, or we assume that he knows we've had a bad day or are exhausted and that a hug will help. But your husband might not be thinking about what you need right then. And so, a real practical step is to simply say to him, "I need a hug."

Honor Your Spouse as Your Brother or Sister in Christ

Notice that we are to "...love as brethren..." (1 Peter 3:8). Before your spouse became your husband or wife, he or she was your brother or sister in the Lord. Right now, in life, God has joined you and your spouse for the purpose of marriage, but when we're all in Heaven, he or she will still be your brother or sister in Christ.

Your spouse deserves the same behavior you would give to anyone in the Body of Christ. You are not going to be ugly with or get into strife with a fellow brother or sister at church. Why? Because this person is your brother or sister in Christ, and he or she deserves your respect.

At times, you must decide to put on the brakes and remind yourself that you are talking to your brother or sister in Christ. It doesn't matter if she's your wife or if he's your husband. It doesn't matter if you're in strife or disagreement with your spouse. She's your sister in Christ. He's your brother in the Lord. As a child of God, he or she deserves respect and honor. Friends, this is really helpful to remember when opportunities for strife arise between the two of you.

Extend Compassion and Courtesy Every Day

At times, your husband or wife may get emotional. First Peter 3:8 declares that we are to "...be pitiful, be courteous...." Your spouse's emotional state may not make sense to you. Rather than correct the person, remember what this verse advises: "Be pitiful." Your spouse may be in a pitiful mood, and they need you. They don't need your correction — they need your pity, love, and compassion.

The next thing this verse instructs us to do is "be courteous." Be polite in your relationship, just as you'd be courteous to anybody else. Remember, you're talking to the most important person in your life other than Jesus. This is your husband or your wife and you should be courteous in your relationship. Denise shared an example of courtesy in action in her marriage to Rick:

> Rick was courteous to me today because I had less time to get ready than he did. I said, "Rick, would you please make the bed?" And he was courteous in saying, "Yes, I'll do that." He was not resentful. He

didn't say, "I don't have time. I don't want to do that." No, he said he would do it and he said it in a very courteous way.

Drawing from the original Greek words contained in First Peter 3:8, the *Renner Interpretive Version* (*RIV*) says:

> **But I have a really important additional, final word. Corporately, all of you are to be synchronized as much as possible in your minds, perceptions, and understanding. You must also be compassionate, sympathetic, and empathetic toward each other, loving each other as those who are actually related to each other — in other words, love like real brothers. You must have emotions for each other so deeply felt that it moves you from a gut level to reach out to do whatever you can to help each other. Be unassuming, unpretentious, having no airs about you. Even if you're more gifted than others, don't be self-promoting, but intentionally think modestly of yourself.**

The Bible tells us to be courteous, to be polite, to be pitiful, to be compassionate, and to love as brethren. First Peter 3:9 says, "Not rendering evil for evil or railing for railing…." These instructions elevate the atmosphere in your marriage. Your spouse is your husband or wife, but also your brother or sister in Christ. As believers, you and your spouse are both Blood-washed individuals and joint-heirs with Christ. In the context of marriage, that brings a lot of honor to the relationship.

In First Corinthians 12:13, God declares that we "have been all made to drink into one Spirit." This verse reveals that even though we're different, we all partake from the same Spirit. We are one, not just because we are married, but because we are one *in Him*.

Esteem One Another and Show Forth God's Love to Your Spouse

This world's system tries to separate us from one another. It causes us to say, "I don't need you. I can do this myself." But not so in the Body of Christ! In His Body, we need one another. Friends, we are to esteem one another because we all receive from the same Spirit.

The *Renner Interpretive Version* (*RIV*) elaborates on First Peter 3:9 as follows:

You absolutely must not try to get even, get revenge, or pay someone back for what he or she did to you or to someone else. Don't try to settle the score by repaying someone for his or her bad, evil, malicious, rotten attitudes and behaviors by exchanging bad, evil, malicious, rotten attitudes and behavior. If someone has verbally abused, berated, damaged, debased, harassed, humiliated, insulted, or misused you or someone else, do not make it your business to pay him or her back with the same kind of verbal abuse. But — on the contrary — that is, on the farthest, opposite end of the spectrum, you must instead speak a blessing in response to that person. For it is for this very purpose that you have been prestigiously called — that you should be the recipients of blessing.

First Peter 3:10 in the King James Version states, "For he that will love life, and see good days, let him refrain his tongue from evil, and his lips that they speak no guile." Taking into consideration the original Greek meaning of this passage, the *Renner Interpretive Version* (*RIV*) of First Peter 3:10 says:

For the person who fully intends to have a life that is full of gusto and zest — that is, a life really worth having and loving — and who wishes to see and personally experience really good and profitable days, times, and seasons in life, let him make sure his tongue refrains and ceases from speaking evil — [if a person wants to have a life filled with gusto and zest — a life really worth having and loving — that is, blessed] — he must purposely put distance between himself and evil. And that includes watching what he says, no longer allowing his mouth to spue [reckless words] or to converse in such a way that baits others and drags them into negative conversations.

We must embrace forgiveness in the context of marriage. Sometimes we just need to *grace* each other. The Bible says that we're to grace each other as God for Christ's sake has graced us. Sometimes the most powerful thing we can do is to give grace to somebody when it's needed. Friend, let's learn to do that in the context of marriage.

STUDY QUESTIONS

Study to shew thyself approved unto God, a workman that needeth not to be ashamed, rightly dividing the word of truth.
— 2 Timothy 2:15

1. In this lesson, we learned not to let corrupt communication proceed out of our mouth. Instead, we're to speak "that which is good to the use of edifying, that it may minister grace unto the hearers." Have you ever been the recipient of someone else's corrupt communication? How did it make you feel? Do you want to ensure that you don't make your spouse feel that way? Then speak words that are good, words that edify, and words that minister *grace* to your spouse. Take time to meditate on the following verses about gracious words.

    - "The words of a wise man's mouth are **gracious,** but the lips of a fool shall swallow him up" (Ecclesiastes 10:12 *NKJV*).

    - **Pleasant words** are like a honeycomb, **sweetness** to the soul and health to the bones" (Proverbs 16:24 *NKJV*).

    - "The thoughts of the wicked are an abomination to the Lord: but the words of the pure are **pleasant words**" (Proverbs 15:26).

    - "A man hath joy by the answer of his mouth: and **a word spoken in due season,** how good is it!" (Proverbs 15:23).

2. How can we be judgmental of anybody else, when we think about how nonjudgmental God has been of us? Think of how God has graced *you.* He has graced you and graced you! Now you are to give grace to others, and that includes your spouse. Sometimes the best thing to do is just overlook something your spouse did and let it go. God has forgiven *you* of everything so you can forgive and give grace to *your spouse.* Read Mark 11:25 (*AMPC*). What adjustments are the Holy Spirit prompting you to make based on this verse? Ask Him to help you make them in Jesus' name.

3. Have you ever thought about the way God's throne is described in the Bible? Hebrews 4:16 says, "Let us therefore come boldly unto the throne **of grace,** that we may obtain mercy, and find grace to help in time of need." What is His throne called? How are we to approach the throne of grace? When should we go to His throne and what will we obtain there? How does it make you feel to know you can go boldly to His throne in your time of need?

PRACTICAL APPLICATION

But be ye doers of the word, and not hearers only,
deceiving your own selves.
—James 1:22

1. When you're talking with your spouse — stop and ask yourself, "Is there a benefit to what I'm saying? Am I going to take my spouse higher or lower by the words I am using?" You may need to find a different way to re-present what you are trying to say. It may benefit you to repackage your words to make them a blessing. Take time to reflect on how you talk with your spouse. Do your words edify and minister grace to your spouse or do your words tear your spouse down instead? Ask the Holy Spirit to help you put a stop to allowing corrupt communication to proceed out of your mouth and ask Him to help you converse with your spouse in a way that edifies and ministers grace to them.

2. Ephesians 4:30 says, "And grieve not the holy Spirit of God, whereby ye are sealed unto the day of redemption." Take time to stop and consider whether your communication with your spouse is blessing the Spirit of God or whether it is grievous to Him. Be honest with yourself and with God. Write down what He reveals to you and change any area that needs correcting.

3. According to First Peter 3:8, you're to be courteous and polite in your relationship with your spouse. You would typically be courteous to anyone else and your spouse is the most important person in your life! This is your husband or your wife. If you're ready to make a fresh commitment to be respectful in your relationship and to give your spouse grace, pray this from your heart: *Father, in the name of Jesus, I thank You that You've given me the power to overlook, let go, and give grace to my spouse. Just as I want people to give me grace, help me to learn that there are moments when I need to close my lips and give grace to other people. Help me to be compassionate, to love my spouse as a brother or sister in Christ, to be pitiful and courteous as First Peter 3 commands. Thank You for it, Father. In Jesus' name. Amen.*

TOPIC

Should You Control Your Mouth?

SCRIPTURES

1. **James 3:5-6** — Even so the tongue is a little member, and boasteth great things. Behold, how great a matter a little fire kindleth! And the tongue is a fire, a world of iniquity: so is the tongue among our members, that it defileth the whole body, and setteth on fire the course of nature; and it is set on fire of hell.

2. **James 3:7-8** — For every kind of beasts, and of birds, and of serpents, and of things in the sea, is tamed, and hath been tamed of mankind: but the tongue can no man tame; it is an unruly evil, full of deadly poison.

3. **James 3:5-8** *(RIV)* — In the same identical way, the tongue is a physically small organ of the body, but in the same way a rudder controls and directs massive ships, the tongue, though small, can make a remarkably big noise and stir a lot of commotion. Think of how remarkable it is that a small fire — if it is kindled sufficiently to re-spark again and again — can stir a fire so great that it can burn down a whole forest! And the tongue is a fire — a world of its own that [if not controlled] is filled with hurt, injustice, wickedness, and violations of every kind. The tongue is positioned right in the middle of our physical organs and [if not controlled] has a defiling, spotting, staining, negative effect on the whole body. If not controlled, it ignites raging passions that, once released, get the wheels moving in a regrettable series of events. Make no mistake, this is a fire that is released from and inflamed by hell itself. For all of nature — including dangerous, ferocious, savage, wild, four-footed beasts, birds, snakes and other reptiles, and things in the sea — are domesticated and tamed, or have been often tamed by the human race. But amazingly, absolutely no one from among mankind is able to control, domesticate, or tame the tongue — for the tongue can be as painful as a thorn bush or prickly plant — a source of chaos, disorder, disturbance, instability, insubordination, unrest, and upheaval. It is a real evil, and it is fully loaded with deadly poison. [Indeed, the untamed tongue looks for opportunities to shoot its arrows of death

at others, and like a poisonous asp or a viper, it waits to strike its next victim and press its fangs down deep enough to release its venom into him. The "venom" is ugly words that produce death in relationships and situations.]

4. **Proverbs 12:18** (*NKJV*) — There is one who speaks like the piercings of a sword, but the tongue of the wise promotes health.

5. **Proverbs 15:28** (*NKJV*) — The heart of the righteous studies how to answer....

6. **Proverbs 15:1** — A soft answer turneth away wrath....

7. **Proverbs 16:23** (*NKJV*) — The heart of the wise teaches his mouth, and adds learning to his lips.

8. **James 1:19** — Wherefore, my beloved brethren, let every man be swift to hear, slow to speak, slow to wrath.

9. **Proverbs 21:23** (*NKJV*) — Whoever guards his mouth and tongue keeps his soul from troubles.

10. **Colossians 4:6** (*NKJV*) — Let your speech always be with grace, seasoned with salt, that you may know how you ought to answer each one.

GREEK WORDS

No Greek words were shown on the TV program.

SYNOPSIS

Our words are so important in our relationships, especially when we are speaking with our spouse. Like a rudder controls a ship, our tongue can steer us into rough, dangerous waters, or it can guide us into calm, smooth sailing seas. The choice is ours. When we allow the Holy Spirit to teach us, we can receive godly wisdom in how to approach every situation. He will guide us in when to listen, when to speak, what to speak, and when to extend grace to our spouse.

The emphasis of this lesson:

Your tongue can be an instrument of healing, or it can be a weapon that brings death — and *you decide* who's going to control your tongue. You must bring your words under the control of the Holy Spirit, particularly in your marriage. By allowing the Holy Spirit to control your tongue

and considering your words before you speak them, your tongue will minister life to your spouse and health to your marriage.

Words Are Powerful, and They Set the Direction of Your Marriage

It's important to control your mouth in your marriage, and that principle applies to every single relationship in life. In James 3:5 and 6, the apostle Paul talked about the tongue. These verses instruct us:

> **Even so the tongue is a little member, and boasteth great things. Behold, how great a matter a little fire kindleth! And the tongue is a fire, a world of iniquity: so is the tongue among our members, that it defileth the whole body, and setteth on fire the course of nature; and it is set on fire of hell.**

Think about how many times you've said something that ignited something terrible in your relationship, and later you were so sorry that you said it. Words are powerful. Words start strife and can even start wars as a result. Verses 7 and 8 go on to declare:

> **For every kind of beasts, and of birds, and of serpents, and of things in the sea, is tamed, and hath been tamed of mankind: but the tongue can no man tame; it is an unruly evil, full of deadly poison.**

Taking into account the original Greek meaning of this passage, the *Renner Interpretive Version (RIV)* of James 3:5–8 says:

> **In the same identical way, the tongue is a physically small organ of the body, but in the same way a rudder controls and directs massive ships, the tongue, though small, can make a remarkably big noise and stir a lot of commotion. Think of how remarkable it is that a small fire — if it is kindled sufficiently to re-spark again and again — can stir a fire so great that it can burn down a whole forest! And the tongue is a fire — a world of its own that [if not controlled] is filled with hurt, injustice, wickedness, and violations of every kind. The tongue is positioned right in the middle of our physical organs and [if not controlled] has a defiling, spotting, staining, negative effect on the whole body. If not controlled, it ignites raging passions that, once released, get the wheels moving in a regrettable series of events. Make**

no mistake, this is a fire that is released from and inflamed by hell itself. For all of nature — including dangerous, ferocious, savage, wild, four-footed beasts, birds, snakes and other reptiles, and things in the sea — are domesticated and tamed, or have been often tamed by the human race. But amazingly, absolutely no one from among mankind is able to control, domesticate, or tame the tongue — for the tongue can be as painful as a thorn bush or prickly plant — a source of chaos, disorder, disturbance, instability, insubordination, unrest, and upheaval. It is a real evil, and it is fully loaded with deadly poison. [Indeed, the untamed tongue looks for opportunities to shoot its arrows of death at others, and like a poisonous asp or a viper, it waits to strike its next victim and press its fangs down deep enough to release its venom into him. The 'venom' is ugly words that produce death in relationships and situations.]

Bring Your Tongue Under Control

How do we guard our words to avoid trouble? Again, James 3:8 declares, "...the tongue can no man tame...." But the good news is that if you submit your tongue to the Holy Spirit, He will help you control — or tame it.

James 3:8 goes on to say the tongue is full of "deadly poison." In the original Greek language, this is expressed by two pictures. One is the picture of somebody pulling back an arrow that's loaded with all kinds of poison. Once the arrow hits its mark, it doesn't just strike — it *poisons*. "Deadly poison" also pictures a poisonous snake that puts its fangs into its victim and then repeatedly pushes those fangs in. And every time it does so, that snake pushes the venom deeper into its victim.

Have you ever been in a situation when somebody began to verbally attack you? They kept pushing and pushing, and you felt like they were trying to put their venom into you. This is one example of the terrible damage poisonous words can do in relationships. You must bring your words under the control of the Holy Spirit. Whether it's in your marriage, or with a sibling, friend, or coworker, bring your tongue under the control of the Holy Spirit. Realize that the words you speak can be an instrument of healing — or they can be a weapon that brings death. And *you decide* what's going to come out of your mouth.

Let the Holy Spirit Teach You What To Say

The tongue can be as sharp as the piercing of a sword. Proverbs 12:18 (*NKJV*) declares, "There is one who speaks like the piercings of a sword, but the tongue of the wise promotes health." Maybe somebody has pierced you with their negative words and you're still trying to get over it, or maybe with your own critical talk you have pierced a sword into somebody else's soul. But in the same verse, we see that "the tongue of the wise promotes health." By making the right choice and submitting ourselves to the Holy Spirit, we can bring health to our hearers.

How do we do this effectively? In Proverbs 15:28 (*NKJV*), we are instructed, "The heart of the righteous studies how to answer...." Controlling the words of our mouth is a process. You must *study* how to answer. You may have to step away from an argument, take control of yourself, and study how you can wisely return to that discussion.

The Holy Spirit is your Teacher and your Guide, the Lover of your soul, and He is right there to instruct you in what you should say. Maybe you shouldn't say anything. Maybe you should say, "I love you so much, and I don't have any more words to say." The Holy Spirit is the One who brings peace. Friend, when you submit yourself and your tongue to Him, He will bring peace into your discussion.

Consider the power of using your words wisely. Proverbs 15:1 (*NKJV*) says, "A soft answer turns away wrath...." If wrath is coming toward you through a person's negative words, a soft answer in response has the power to rebuke wrath. Your soft words spoken in kindness have more power than that wrath because you are coming from the place of listening to the Holy Spirit. You are joined with the Holy Spirit and in a position of confidence because of Him. So when you come back into that discussion with a soft answer, wrath is turned away.

Think About Where Your Words Will Take You Before You Speak

In relationships, when you're in a conversation that can be difficult, it is wise to do more thinking than you do talking. James 3:4 and 5 (*NKJV*) instructs, "Look also at ships: although they are so large and are driven by fierce winds, they are turned by a very small rudder wherever the pilot desires. Even so the tongue is a little member and boasts great things."

The tongue is like the rudder of a ship. Wherever the rudder is pointed, that's where the ship will go, and our words are like this as well. If we set our tongue to speak something that is spiteful or harsh, it will lead us into really rough waters.

Before we speak, we must determine where we want to go in our relationship. Do we want peace? Do we desire to sail into clear, peaceful waters? Stop and think about where your words are going to take you. If you are in a conversation with your spouse, consider how you will answer before you open your mouth. Thinking before speaking allows you to filter your words according to God's wisdom. Saying anything that comes into your mind right away will always lead to trouble.

There are many pauses in conversations where you can consider how to say something. Ask yourself: *Should I say this? Will there be a benefit to me saying it? Do I need to rephrase my words and say this in a different way? How would I feel if someone said it to me?* Pause, think, and surrender your tongue to the Holy Spirit. Realize you have an opportunity for your tongue to work like a rudder — bringing healing and help or taking you and your spouse into rougher waters.

You don't need to say everything fast, all at once. It is better to *slow down*, submit your thoughts to the Spirit of God, and choose your words carefully. Make sure you are going to say something that will minister grace to the hearer and be helpful rather than destructive. In marriage, sometimes you need to be more silent than talkative. Pause and think, *really think*, about what you're going to say before you say it.

Teach Your Mouth Wisely

The Bible admonishes us in Proverbs 16:23 (*NKJV*), "The heart of the wise teaches his mouth, and adds learning to his lips." Being wise in controlling our tongue involves a teaching process. Make a declaration over your mouth and instruct it by saying: "Mouth, I'm teaching you right now. You are not going to say that. Instead, you will say this."

Friend, the Holy Spirit inside of us is the Greater One. This means He is the Greater One over any situation — *if we yield to Him*. When we come in line with the Holy Spirit, we can teach our mouth not to bring destruction to our conversation. We can choose to bring peace instead. This is the kind of power we have with the help of the Holy Spirit to correct our speech.

Be quick to hear the Holy Spirit speaking to you. James 1:19 tells us, "Wherefore, my beloved brethren, let every man be swift to hear, slow to speak, slow to wrath." The Holy Spirit will probably tell you to *slow down* and listen. The very next thing this verse says is to be "slow to speak." The word "slow" here in the Greek describes *a person who has an impediment*. They don't have the ability to speak fast. They have a hard time getting their words out. Rather than rushing to release a slew of words you'll regret, choose to have a hard time getting those words out — be "slow to speak" like the Word of God instructs.

The verse then says to be "slow to wrath." Being slow to speak and slow to wrath are connected because wrath and speech are connected. When you say things you don't like, spewing vile words, it's connected to your wrath. Your wrath follows because you stirred it up. That's how powerful the tongue is.

Decide that you will be "swift to hear." Slow down and choose to hear what God is saying to you. Be quiet and listen to what your spouse is saying. Sometimes, we can think so much about what we're going to say next that we don't hear what's being communicated. But you *must* hear what's being communicated, so choose to close your mouth, listen well, and after you hear, be slow in your response. If you're slow to speak, you'll also be slow to wrath. You can put on the brakes by choosing to control your mouth.

Guard Your Mouth To Keep Yourself From Trouble

Proverbs 21:23 (*NKJV*) says, "Whoever guards his mouth and tongue keeps his soul from troubles." Notice that to keep our soul from troubles, we must do something specific with our mouth and tongue. As we obey the Bible by guarding our mouth and teaching our tongue, we keep ourselves from trouble and our soul is protected.

For 16 years, Denise has taught thousands of women about marriage, both online as well as face to face. She shared this testimony of how controlling our words can create peace and prevent trouble with our spouse:

> One day, I was teaching the ladies about controlling their mouth and I said, 'Don't criticize, don't complain, and don't correct.' One of the women I taught went home and did what I said the whole

week. She kept her mouth closed from correcting, criticizing, and teaching. She came back the next Sunday and said, 'This was the most peaceful week that I've ever had in my marriage.'

Why did this woman have the most peaceful week she's ever had in her marriage? Because she guarded her words. And what happened when she guarded her words? It kept her soul from trouble! A lot of times we say, "My mouth is just out of control." No, it's not out of control — with the help of the Holy Spirit, we can bring our tongue under control.

Minister Healing With Your Words

Colossians 4:6 (*NKJV*) teaches, "Let your speech always be with grace, seasoned with salt, that you may know how you ought to answer each one." Salt is used for healing. Consider your words and recognize whether they are going to bring healing or trouble. This is powerful! We can stop so much strife and trouble simply by controlling our mouth.

How many times have you been in a conversation, had a negative thought, and you've said to yourself, "I shouldn't say that." But then you did say it, and it's like venom was injected through your words into your victim. It immediately brought a bad result, and you wished you had listened to what the Holy Spirit was telling you and kept that thought to yourself. You wished you could take those words back, but it was too late.

In a case like that, here is what to do. Stop immediately and minister words seasoned with salt. Say, "You know what? I shouldn't have said that. That was harsh and unkind and not helpful. Would you please forgive me for saying that?" Do what you can to bring healing to a bad situation that you created with your own mouth. God has given you so much power to bring healing to others instead of destruction.

Friend, you are the one with authority over your mouth. You can't blame your spouse and say, "My spouse made me say that." No, they didn't — you made the choice to say that. But now you can *make the choice to bring healing*. Proverbs 18:21 says, "Death and life are in the power of the tongue: and they that love it shall eat the fruit thereof." By the power of the Holy Spirit, you can choose to have life and healing and blessing coming out of your mouth. In this way, you'll bless your spouse and create peace within your marriage.

STUDY QUESTIONS

**Study to shew thyself approved unto God, a workman that needeth
not to be ashamed, rightly dividing the word of truth.**
— 2 Timothy 2:15

1. In this lesson, we learned how powerful the tongue is. The Bible calls
    our tongue "a fire, a world of iniquity" (James 3:6) and "an unruly
    evil full of deadly poison" (James 3:8). It's vital to the health of our
    marriage that we control our tongue. As believers, with the help of the
    Holy Spirit, we can tame our tongue. What kind of impact might it
    make if we take time to meditate daily on scriptures that will help us
    bridle our tongue which the Lord gave us to steward? Consider:

    *   "Set a guard, O Lord, over **my mouth**; keep watch over the door of
        my lips" (Psalm 141:3 *NKJV*).

    *   "Let the **words** of my mouth, and the meditation of my heart, be
        acceptable in thy sight, O Lord, my strength, and my Redeemer"
        (Psalm 19:14).

    *   "In the multitude of **words** sin is not lacking, but he who restrains
        his **lips** is wise" (Proverbs 10:19 *NKJV*).

    *   "I will bless the Lord at all times: His praise shall continually be in
        my mouth" (Psalm 34:1).

    *   "…The Lord God has given Me **the tongue** of a disciple and of one
        who is taught, that I should know how to speak **a word in season** to
        him who is weary. He wakens Me morning by morning, He wakens My
        ear to hear as a disciple [as one who is taught] (Isaiah 50:4 *AMPC*).

2. In the program, Denise shared that when she teaches women on mar-
    riage, she encourages them to control their mouth. She instructs them,
    saying, "Don't criticize. Don't correct, and don't complain." By doing
    what Denise taught, a woman testified that she had the most peaceful
    week she's ever had in her marriage! What are some additional ways
    you can bring peace into *your* home? (*See* Romans 15:13; 2 Corinthi-
    ans 13:11; Philippians 4:4–7; and Colossians 3:15.)

3. It is vital to bring your mouth under the control of the Holy Spirit
    and realize that your words are either used as an instrument of healing
    or a weapon that brings death. As a believer, you can submit your
    tongue to the Holy Spirit, and wonderful things will result! What

new insights about your words are you receiving from the Holy Spirit in the following verses?

- "The mouth of a righteous man is a well of life…" (Proverbs 10:11).
- "A man hath joy by the answer of his mouth: and a word spoken in due season, how good is it!" (Proverbs 15:23).
- "…The mouth of the upright shall deliver them" (Proverbs 12:6).
- "He that keepeth his mouth keepeth his life: but he that openeth wide his lips shall have destruction" (Proverbs 13:3).

PRACTICAL APPLICATION

**But be ye doers of the word, and not hearers only,
deceiving your own selves.
—James 1:22**

1. Reread this lesson on controlling your mouth and allow the weight of it to penetrate your heart and mind. Ask the Holy Spirit to help you put this lesson into practice and thank God in advance for the results you will see from being a "doer" of the Word of God. Which passages of Scripture from this lesson stood out to you? Write them down and meditate on them daily. Allow them to change you and write down the fruit you're seeing in your life because of the changes you've made in controlling your mouth. Glory to God!

2. Have you ever thought about the fact that God gave each of us *two* ears and *one* mouth? If we could allow that to remind us to do twice as much listening as we do talking, imagine how that could positively affect our marriage and more! In James 1:9, the Bible tells us to be "swift to hear, slow to speak, slow to wrath." Today, get in a quiet place and consecrate yourself before the Lord. Make a quality decision to be *quick to hear* what the Holy Spirit says to you. Next, reflect on how much listening — *real listening* — you do in your marriage. Choose to be a better listener moving forward and value the things your spouse has to say. Then ask the Holy Spirit to help you be *slow* to speak — to use your tongue to bring healing and life to your spouse and marriage.

3. You and your spouse are more than just a married couple — you're partners in fulfilling your God-given purpose! Nurture your marriage as you've learned in these lessons. With the help of the Holy Spirit, intentionally:

- Keep Christ at the center.
- Fulfill God's purpose together.
- Shut the door to strife.
- Give each other grace.
- Control your mouth.

Value your marriage — don't throw it away. *Value* your spouse, and the covenant God gave you. Focus on the good qualities your spouse has instead of the bad ones. You may have made mistakes, but the Lord's restorative power is available for you right now! There is always hope. Allow the Holy Spirit to strengthen and encourage your heart regarding your marriage. You *can* have a happy marriage, in Jesus' name! (*See* 1 John 1:7,9; Joel 2:25; Philippians 4:6-8; Luke 1:37.)

A Prayer To Receive Salvation

If you've never received Jesus as your Savior and Lord, now is the time for you to experience the new life Jesus wants to give you! To receive God's gift of salvation that can be obtained through Jesus alone, pray this prayer from your heart:

Jesus, I repent of my sin and receive You as my Savior and Lord. Wash away my sin with Your precious blood and make me completely new. I thank You that my sin is removed, and Satan no longer has any right to lay claim on me. Through Your empowering grace, I faithfully promise that I will serve You as my Lord for the rest of my life.

If you just prayed this prayer of salvation, you are born again! You are a brand-new creation in Christ! Would you please let us know of your decision by going to **renner.org/salvation**? We would love to connect with you and pray for you as you begin your new life in Christ.

Scriptures for further study: John 3:16; John 14:6; Acts 4:12; Ephesians 1:7; Hebrews 10:19,20; 1 Peter 1:18,19; Romans 10:9,10; Colossians 1:13; 2 Corinthians 5:17; Romans 6:4; 1 Peter 1:3

Notes

CLAIM YOUR FREE RESOURCE!

As a way of introducing you further to the teaching ministry of Rick Renner, we would like to send you FREE of charge his teaching, "How To Receive a Miraculous Touch From God" on CD or as an MP3 download.

How To Receive a Miraculous Touch From God
Rick Renner

CD36

RENNER

In His earthly ministry, Jesus commonly healed *all* who were sick of *all* their diseases. In this profound message, learn about the manifold dimensions of Christ's wisdom, goodness, power, and love toward all humanity who came to Him in faith with their needs.

☑ YES, I want to receive Rick Renner's monthly teaching letter!

Simply scan the QR code to claim this resource or go to: **renner.org/claim-your-free-offer**

Connect

WITH US!

R renner.org

f facebook.com/rickrenner • facebook.com/rennerdenise

▶ youtube.com/rennerministries • youtube.com/deniserenner

◉ instagram.com/rickrrenner • instagram.com/rennerministries_
instagram.com/rennerdenise

www.ingramcontent.com/pod-product-compliance
Lightning Source LLC
Chambersburg PA
CBHW071642040426
42452CB00009B/1731